It's Disgusting—and We Ate It!

True Food Facts from Around the World— and Throughout History!

Hairy weeds for breakfast,
slippery snakes for lunch,
scary blobs that grow at night,
and bowls of bloody punch—

with such a lovely dinner
how could I ever wish
for candy bars and chocolate cake
and ice cream in my dish?

by James Solheim
illustrated by Eric Brace

Aladdin Paperbacks
New York   London   Toronto   Sydney   Singapore

First Aladdin Paperbacks edition July 2001
Text copyright © 1998 by James Solheim
Illustrations copyright © 1998 by Eric Brace.
Aladdin Paperbacks
An imprint of Simon & Schuster
Children's Publishing Division
1230 Avenue of the Americas
New York, NY 10020
Also available in a Simon & Schuster Books for Young Readers hardcover edition
Designed by Edward Miller
The text for this book was set in 12-pt. Stone Informal.
Printed and bound in Singapore
10 9 8 7 6 5 4 3 2 1
The Library of Congress has cataloged the hardcover edition as follows:
Solheim, James.
It's disgusting—and we ate it! : True food facts from around the world and throughout history! / James Solheim : Eric Brace, illustrator.
p.   cm.   Includes bibliographic references.
Summary: A collection of poems, facts, statistics, and stories about unusual foods and eating habits both contemporary and historical.
ISBN: 0-689-80675-2 (hc.)
1. Food—Juvenile literature. 2. Food—History—Juvenile history. 3. Food habits—Juvenile literature. 4. Food habits—History—Juvenile literature. [1. Food. 2. Food—History.
3. Food habits—History.] I. Brace, Eric, ill. II. Title.
TX355.S648 1997 641.3—dc20 96-7406
ISBN: 0-689-84393-3 (Aladdin pbk.)

CONTENTS

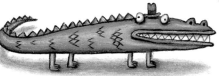

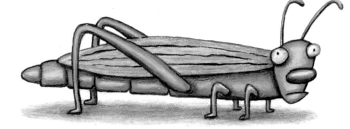

SOMETHING'S MOVING IN MY LUNCH BOX

What would you rather eat for lunch—a steaming piece of pizza, a bowl of bugs, a live oyster, or a fish's head?

You might be surprised to learn that many people in the world would not answer "PIZZA!"

In Europe and Asia, many kids love to eat fish heads. Americans gulp down tons of live oysters a day. And many Africans know that a properly cooked grasshopper has a delightful crunch.

What's disgusting and what's delicious? It depends on where you live and what you're used to eating. It depends on whether the refrigerator has been invented yet and whether your mom once got sick eating tomatoes. It depends on many things—maybe on everything that ever happened up to the moment you lifted that fork.

So grab a cockroach cookie and turn the page for some of the sickest, silliest, and strangest meals the world has ever known. When you're done, maybe you'll have a hankering for something really horrid—like spinach!

PART ONE
People Eat the Wildest Things
Adventures in the World's Weirdest and Funniest Foods

FROG LEGS

(EUROPE, AMERICA, AND ELSEWHERE)

Imagine yourself slurping a soup full of tadpoles or finding a stuffed frog nestled in your rice.

Today, most frog meat comes from the legs. But if you had lived centuries ago, tadpoles and whole frogs might have been your favorite foods!

Frogs live in most of the world's countries. They are the only amphibians that live north of the Arctic Circle. Many people buy frog meat at gourmet grocery stores, but adventurous eaters can hunt their own in lakes and ponds.

JUST SHUT YOUR EYES AND THINK OF CHICKEN

Everyone says they taste like chicken—
    that fried in butter they're juicy lickin'.
They say if I'd just *try* a bite
    I'd end up eating the whole dang night

(gulping them down like candy bars).
Well, I don't care if movie stars
    come and feed them to me on toast.
I'll never convince myself the roast-

ed jiggle on my tongue is meat
    the human mouth was meant to eat.
And don't try hiding it in stew—
    I'll know it's *frog* whatever you do!

AND NOW... a poem.

FROG Legs make me CROAK!

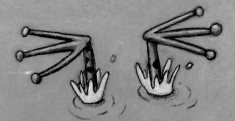

2

Three Famous Words

"Tastes Like Chicken!"

Whether it's with frog legs, alligator tails, or another offbeat meat, these three words keep coming back like a bad aftertaste.

Here are some spicier comparisons people have made to describe their favorite freaky foods.

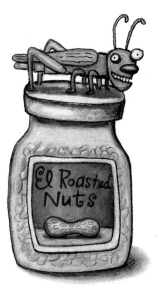

Boiled cattail shoots taste like asparagus.

Dulse (a type of seaweed) tastes like lightly salted nuts.

Prickly pear cactus fruits taste like raspberries.

Dry-roasted crickets taste like smoked nuts.

Salted earthworms taste like beef jerky.

Fried wax moth caterpillars taste like bacon.

Giant spiders from Venezuela taste like crab.

Giant spiders from New Guinea taste like peanut butter.

Fried flour beetle larvae taste like sunflower seeds.

Witchetty grubs (insect larvae) taste like sweet scrambled eggs.

Rat meat tastes like pork.

Alligator meat tastes like lobster.

Friday Is Frog Day

In the Middle Ages, on days when European Catholics weren't supposed to eat any meat but fish, they could still eat frog and beaver meat. If it swam, they thought, it must be a fish!

EARTHWORM SOUP

(CHINA AND ELSEWHERE)

In China, earthworm soup is a traditional fever medicine. But the Chinese aren't alone in their use of this high-protein, low-fat food. The French, Aztecs, and Vietnamese have all eaten worms at different times in history.

The worm has even played a royal role. Long ago, in a New Zealand tribe called the Maori, no one was allowed to eat certain earthworms but the chief—except as a last meal. Today worm-eaters in Australia enjoy long white worms dug from rotten logs and eaten raw.

ANTICIPATION

O
mouthfuls
of
squirmy
squiggly
mucky
loop the
loops! a
royal feast
if you
waited
your
whole
life
to taste
slimy
grimy
greasy
lapping
pails of
tails

SIDEWINDER SALAD

(THE AMERICAN WEST)

It's not easy making mincemeat of a rattlesnake. The snake's many tiny ribs make the meat hard to extract. And a six-pound snake might have only a pound or so of meat on its body.

One restaurant buys skinned whole snakes (minus the head and rattles) from a snake farm in Texas. Chefs cook the snake, skeleton and all. Next they hand-peel the meat from the bones. Then they add spices and arrange the meat on a bed of mixed greens, crafting the snake into a delightful eating experience.

A poem.

I SHOULD HAVE ASKED FOR TUNA CASSEROLE

fast-lashing teeth and tattletale tail.
deadly at one end. delicious on down—

dear rattlesnake, my dangerous dinner.
don't do to me what I do to you

Good Snakey.

Snake Bites

• Poison from animal bites and stings is called venom. In rattlesnakes, venom is found only in sacs connected to the fangs, not in the meat.

• In China and France, people often called snakes "hedge eels" or "brushwood eels." Apparently the thought of eating snakes was too much for some people, but eels—they were yummy!

• Rattlesnake is lower in fat than most of the meats you already enjoy. It's a tender white meat with a mild flavor and texture like that of crab. What's so scary about that?

INSECTS

(MOST COUNTRIES)

The Australian honey ant stores so much of a sugary fluid in its body that its hind end swells to a globe big enough to eat. People bite the bug's end off to get at the sweet stuff inside. It's almost the same as eating honey from bees—but with an extra touch of insect flavor.

Termites are a gourmet food to many Africans. People eat fried grasshoppers in many parts of Asia, Africa, and the Middle East, and pioneer Americans boiled locusts in soup. The famous Greek philosopher Aristotle said that cicadas taste best with their eggs inside of them.

I want termites.

I want GRUBS.

I want a poem.

BOBWHITE, BOBWHITE,
WHAT SHALL WE EAT TONIGHT?

Silkworm pizza, grubs in pies,
caterpillars and termite fries—

who will eat them?
Whippoorwill

and so will I.

Fried grasshoppers, locust stew,
candied crickets with honeydew—

who tried such treats?
Katydid

and I did too!

Pile on That Protein

Spiders and flies may not look like much, but as protein providers they're at the top of the heap.

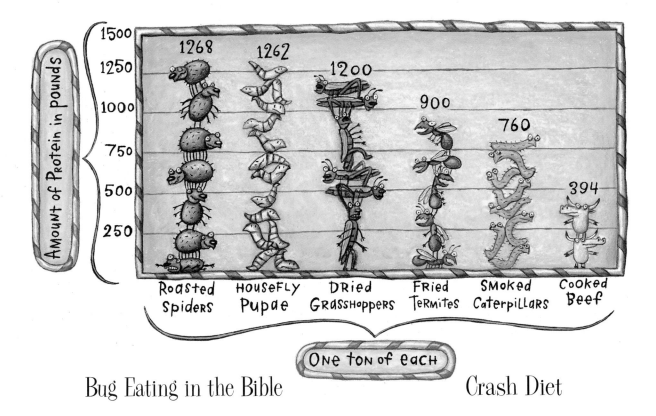

Amount of Protein in Pounds

1500 | 1250 | 1000 | 750 | 500 | 250

1268 — Roasted Spiders
1262 — Housefly Pupae
1200 — Dried Grasshoppers
900 — Fried Termites
760 — Smoked Caterpillars
394 — Cooked Beef

One ton of each

Bug Eating in the Bible

"John [the Baptist]'s clothes were made of camel's hair. . . . His food was locusts and wild honey."

(Matthew 3: 4)

"There are . . . some winged creatures that walk on all fours that you may eat: those that have jointed legs for hopping on the ground. Of these you may eat any kind of locust, katydid, cricket, or grasshopper. But all other winged creatures that have four legs you are to detest."

(Leviticus 11: 21–23)

Crash Diet

When U.S. Air Force Captain Scott O'Grady's plane went down in 1995 during the war in Bosnia, he had to eat ants to survive. He smashed them against his backpack and ate them raw. After he had survived for six days on sour ants, grass, and leaves, rescuers found him. Guess what he did as soon as he got on the rescue chopper? Eat, of course!

7

FLOWER SALAD

(MANY COUNTRIES WORLDWIDE)

In a world where flowers can be poison, you might be surprised to learn that some blooms have satisfied stomachs for centuries.

England's royalty ate violets in salad, candy, and hare stew. Ancient Romans cooked rose petals with animal brains to make pudding. And America had no dandelions till immigrants brought them from Europe. People fry the petals in pancakes and eat the young leaves in salad or scrambled eggs.

Dandelion scrambled eggs? Yuck!

I guess eating eggs is a little gross now that you mention it.

And now a perfumed poem.

SOME CALL IT A BOUQUET

My love gave me a single white rose
My love gave me a dandelion's glow
My love gave me the violets' dew

so I made a salad

The Gold Mine in the Garden

Saffron, the world's costliest spice, comes from flowers. Workers remove three tiny tips from a type of crocus blossom to make the spice. It takes 225,000 tips to make one pound of saffron. Because this work takes so much time, a pound can cost up to $4,000.

Medieval kings and queens loved saffron, as do Middle Eastern cooks today. Sometimes people paid more for this golden spice than they did for gold itself!

Stronger Than the Strongest Orange

Oranges, lemons, and limes are our most famous sources of vitamin C. But some of the most powerful sources might be found in your backyard.

Amount of Vitamin C in pounds

35 30 25 20 15 10 5 0

Rose Hips   Violet Leaves   Wild Garlic Mustard   Oranges

One ton of Each

Eat Like a King, Burp Like a King

Some ancient copies of this recipe call for over a dozen strong herbs including garlic and onion—but no lettuce or spinach. Talk about a royal case of bad breath!

We bow to you out of Respect, and 'cause your Breath makes us woozy.

EEERRP

Salad

(from an English royal recipe over 500 years old)

Peel, wash, chop, and tear up fresh herbs from the list below, using only a little of each. Then add lots of spinach and leaf lettuce. Toss with olive oil. Add a dash of vinegar and salt.

LEEK   SAGE
GARLIC   WATERCRESS
ONION   FENNEL
GREEN ONION   EDIBLE FLOWERS
CHIVES   INCLUDING ROSES AND
PARSLEY   ENGLISH VIOLETS
MINT

NOTE: Get a grownup's help and use only flowers that were grown for food. Do not use wild plants of any kind unless you have learned from an expert how to avoid poisonous look-alikes. If you can't find edible flowers at a food store, the other items in the list will do fine.

SEAWEED

(MOST COUNTRIES)

On the island of Fiji, people eat crunchy seaweed mixed with fermented coconut milk. East Coast Canadians eat seaweed snacks instead of potato chips. In fact, almost everybody who lives by the sea eats ocean vegetables. And these underwater treats find their way onto more inland tables every day.

...AND NOW, a poem for BiRdBRains.

IN MY SALAD SEA

in my salad sea
i'll swim and dream
and eat seaweed
with oyster cream

and pick my teeth
with a seahorse tail
and ride to dinner
on a whale

oh, i'll never need
to leave the sea—
where the fish are fresh
and the salad's free

Space Slime

Experiments have shown that a slimy relative of seaweed could serve as food in outer space. The plants would grow on space explorers' waste products, providing food and oxygen in return.

You Have Already Eaten Seaweed

Do you have ice cream in your freezer? If so, pull it out, brush off those ice crystals, and read the ingredients list on the container. You'll find *carrageenan* in the recipe for most ice cream sold in America. Carrageenan comes from a kind of seaweed often called Irish moss.

Many foods contain seaweed products. The sea's best weeds often show up in frozen foods, cakes, pies, and brand-name toppings like hot fudge and salad dressing. Look for *agar*, *carrageenan*, and *alginates* on the labels of your favorite foods. You might find out you just ate seaweed for lunch.

I thought you didn't like seafood.

This is one seafood I can really sink my teeth into.

Pond Scum It's Not

These edible seaweeds sound just as bad as the poisonous kinds:

BLADDER WRACK
GRAPESTONE
SEA OTTER'S CABBAGE
SPONGE TANG

HORSETAIL TANGLE
SEA NOODLE
COW HAIR
MERMAID'S FISHING LINE

STAR JELLY
FAIRIES' BUTTER
SEA LETTUCE
SUGAR WRACK

Stone Soup

Starving people can be pretty creative at finding food—even eating the crust from rocks. A lichen called *rock tripe* makes an unusual soup, and another bitter lichen gives Icelanders a nutritious flour. Rock tripe fed George Washington's starving troops at Valley Forge.

Lichen is actually two kinds of things growing together— fungi and tiny plants related to seaweed. By teaming up, they thrive where very few plants can live. It's two gross foods in one!

Have you ever caught a SHARK by mistake?

No—but I caught one on PORPOISE.

SUSHI

(JAPAN)

Sushi is the name for a wide range of Japanese rice dishes often based on raw fish. Sushi chefs can be real artists, making food that looks pretty enough to hang on the wall.

But raw fish isn't the only tool of the sushi artist. Seaweed, raw squid, and other ocean foods add to the sushi master's palette. In a crowded country with little land and lots of ocean, people learn to create with creatures from the sea.

And NOW, a poem.*

SEASON OF INVENTION

Whoops   I plum forgot
to fry this fish   Forgive me
I was spring dreaming

BLess You.

Do You Need a tissue?

Haiku

Would You Like Fries with That?

Japanese people could buy "fast-food" sushi as early as 1680—hundreds of years before the world's first burger place opened.

*This poem is a haiku. Invented in Japan, a haiku is a descriptive three-line poem that expresses a moment's complex emotion and insight. The first and last lines have five syllables, and the middle line has seven syllables.

Something's Rotten in Rome

What's worse—fresh raw fish or fish left out to spoil? In the hands of amateurs, both can be dangerous. But people have learned how to use even the food with the most famous stink—rotten fish.

CHA
(Ancient Chinese)

Left to spoil in a milk preparation, different types of fish developed their own, shall we say, *peculiar* smells and tastes. Aristocrats ate cha as a paste or in petal-thin slices.

Hmmm... I believe this needs more fish guts.

RAKØRRET
(Modern Norwegians)

After several months in salt and sugar, a dead trout gets good and ripe. Sometimes a bit too ripe!

P. U.

GARUM
(Ancient Romans)

Two thousand years ago, salty rotten fish guts were an important part of most gourmet foods.

Okay, joke's over. Get me outta here.

salt

NUOC MAM
(Modern Vietnamese)

Fish buried in salt eventually digest themselves—with their own stomach fluids. The resulting sauce seasons many foods.

Czar's Choice

Would you pay $900 for a one-pound jar of fish eggs taken from a live fish? That's today's rate for the best caviar.

Caviar made from golden sterlet eggs was so prized that at one time only the czar of Russia was allowed to eat it.

May I help you?

Yes, I'd like some flour, some sugar, some soda pop and two pounds of caviar.

BOB

BIRD'S-NEST SOUP

(CHINA)

One small region of Southeast Asia provides the whole world's supply of nests for bird's-nest soup. Men climb three hundred feet up vines and bamboo poles and risk their lives to harvest the nests of birds called *swiftlets*. These birds fly into huge caves to make nests with their own spit. But the birds are becoming more rare because people steal too many of their nests.

At over $1,000 a pound, these nests of hardened spit are among the world's most costly foods.

TREASURE OF THE CAVE

I climbed a cliff
            on a bamboo pole
and stole
            some nests (the birds made more)

I stirred them in
            a boiling brew
for stew

(mmmm—how sweet and true.

        to smile and swallow
        a swiftlet's squishy spittle.
        to sip her gourmet glue)

That's Some Spitwad

A hundred tons of dainty little birds' nests go into Hong Kong's soup pots every year—more than the weight of a thousand people.

14

More Than Just Egg Rolls

Bird's-nest soup gives us just a taste of how daring China's cooks have been over the centuries. Here are some of that vast land's wilder dishes—from ancient royal favorites like owl to the dried jellyfish still enjoyed today.

Barbecued Elephant's Trunk

Chicken Red (boiled chicken blood)

Dragon, Phoenix, and Tiger (Actually snake, chicken, and cat)

Baked Owl

White Tree Ears (A kind of fungus)

Camel Hump Stew

Breast of Panther

Sliced Python in Vinegar

Dried Jellyfish

Bear Paw Cooked in a gob of Clay

Thousand-year-old Eggs Cured in Mud (Actually several months to several years old)

Tiger Bone Liquor

Tartar Sauce

Over seven hundred years ago, a wandering Asian people called the *Tartars* could go for ten days without gathering food or using any food they had packed. How did they do it?

They pricked the veins of their horses and drank the blood. Since horses are so large, a Tartar mealtime hardly slowed the animals down.

PART TWO
From Mammoth Meatballs to Squirrel Stew
Hairy, Scary Foods Throughout History

WOOLLY MAMMOTH MEAT
(NORTHERN HEMISPHERE)

Woolly mammoths must have seemed like monsters to prehistoric people. Yet early hunters overcame their fear of mammoths' fang-like tusks and had their monsters for dinner.

Most mammoths died more than ten thousand years ago, but a few dwarf mammoths lived at least until the time of the Egyptian pyramids. In modern times, people still sometimes find woolly mammoths frozen in the mud of Siberia, where they died thousands of years ago.

tusk, tusk, a poem.

THEY WERE MONSTERS, I TELL YOU. MONSTERS

a mob of monsters came grumbling along

an earthquake of monsters

five-foot fur
fifteen-foot fangs

long grabbing noses
i thought they might GET US

what could we *do?*
what could we DO?

run? scream? faint?

(we ate 'em)

Scientists Tempted to Eat 40,000-Year-Old Mammoth!

"The flesh from under the shoulder, fibrous and marbled with fat, is dark red and looks as fresh as well-frozen beef or horse meat. It looked so appetising that we wondered for some time whether we would not taste it. But no one would venture to take it into his mouth, and horseflesh was given the preference.

The dogs ate whatever mammoth meat we threw them."

—Dr. Otto F. Hertz, October 17, 1901
(scientist digging a frozen woolly mammoth from the mud along the Beresovka River in northern Russia)

Ancient Foods We Could Still Eat—If We Dared

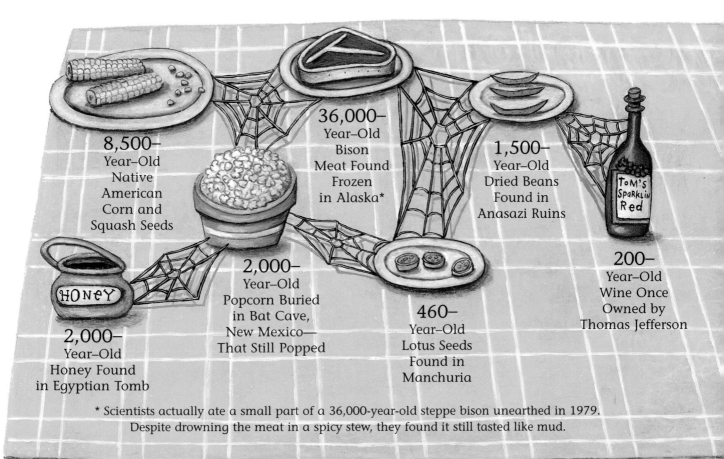

8,500–Year-Old Native American Corn and Squash Seeds

36,000–Year-Old Bison Meat Found Frozen in Alaska*

1,500–Year-Old Dried Beans Found in Anasazi Ruins

2,000–Year-Old Honey Found in Egyptian Tomb

2,000–Year-Old Popcorn Buried in Bat Cave, New Mexico—That Still Popped

460–Year-Old Lotus Seeds Found in Manchuria

200–Year-Old Wine Once Owned by Thomas Jefferson

* Scientists actually ate a small part of a 36,000-year-old steppe bison unearthed in 1979. Despite drowning the meat in a spicy stew, they found it still tasted like mud.

SEEDS, MICE, AND INSECTS

(THE ANASAZI)

The Anasazi people lived for thousands of years in the American Southwest. About seven hundred years ago, they mysteriously abandoned many of their towns. Nobody knows exactly why they left, but we do know what they ate—because the desert preserved pieces of their digestive waste (called *coprolites* when they get old and stonelike). Scientists dissolved the coprolites to free the hard parts of the food the Anasazi had swallowed, which included insects and small animals like pack rats and mice (bones, fur, and all).

DESERT MYSTERY

we   the Anasazi   left you clues

                    a charred note   (written in seeds)

an eternal fist   (grain-grinding stone)

          we wrote our lives in shells hulls spines bones

hard things that passed right through
and stayed to speak of us when we passed on too

This Isn't Food—It's a Fish!

If you think the Anasazi were strange for enjoying a tasty mouse stew while refusing to eat fish, consider this. Most Americans today enjoy fish while refusing to eat rabbit—which English kings liked so much they had it served at royal feasts.

Tastes change over the ages. If history had been different, modern Americans might have hated these everyday foods that have appalled people yesterday and today.

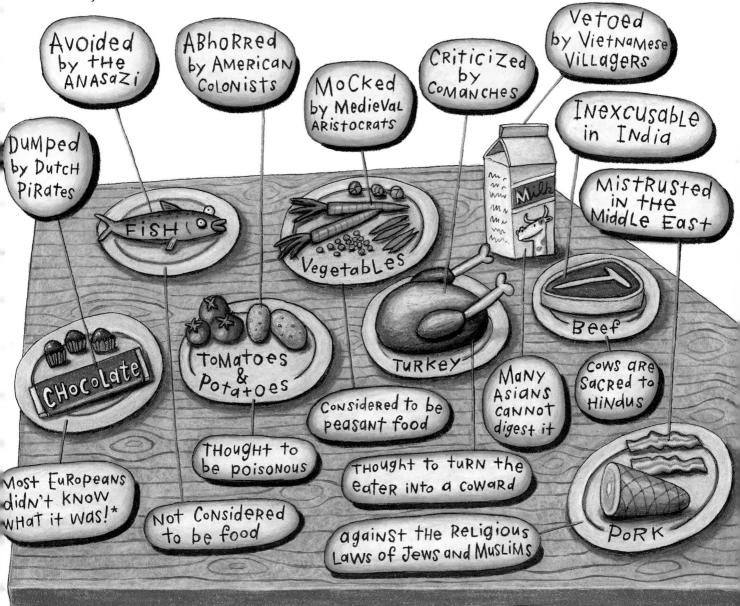

*Long ago, when Dutch pirates found a load of chocolate on a ship they had raided, they threw it overboard in disgust. The Spanish and Portuguese had kept chocolate a secret from the rest of Europe. The pirates didn't know they were throwing away a delicious treat from the Americas!

A ROYAL FEAST

(MEDIEVAL ENGLAND)

Royal food in old England may have been exotic, but it didn't provide a balanced diet. Ancient royalty ate far too much meat.

Most of the guests used a piece of stale bread for a plate. And when a servant brought a bowl of soup, the guests sometimes plunged their arms in up to the elbows to get at juicy morsels. Afterward, they threw their scraps into a pot for the poor.

And now a Royal poem for Royal appetites.

OUR KING FILLS TWO THRONES

jellied crayfish, pails of eels,
seagulls, whales, meat from seals,

peacock roasts in their feathers and skins,
swans and larks and things with fins—

so many glorious foods amassed
that when the feasting's done at last

a wagon rolls to the royal store
filled with scraps to feed the poor

A Bowl of Hot, Tasty Garbage from the Sewer

One fancy soup served at royal feasts was called "garbage." It was made with birds' heads, feet, livers, necks, and gizzards. Soup was often called "sewe" and the server was called the "sewer."

Just think how often kings must have shouted to their servants, "Get some garbage from the sewer and bring it for my dinner!"

Eat Yourself Sick, Your Highness

In medieval times, the amount of food served at royal feasts was often staggering. This is a list of food bought for a feast in 1387:

14 oxen lying in salt
2 oxen, fresh
120 heads of sheep, fresh
120 carcasses of sheep, fresh
12 boars
14 calves
140 piglets
300 marrow bones
lard and grease, enough
3 tons of salt venison
3 does of fresh venison
50 swans

210 geese
50 capons of high grease
8 dozen other capons
60 dozen hens
200 pair rabbits
4 pheasants
5 herons and bitterns*
6 young goats
5 dozen young hens for jelly
12 dozen young hens to roast
100 dozen pigeons
12 dozen partridges

8 dozen young rabbits
10 dozen curlews*
12 dozen whimbrels*
12 cranes
wild fowl, enough
120 gallons milk
12 gallons cream
40 gallons of curds
3 bushels of apples
11 thousand eggs

*types of birds

All RiGHt NoW, WHat's foR desseRt?

Shakespeare's Crazy Cupboard

In William Shakespeare's famous play *King Lear*, a character named Edgar pretends to be a madman who eats all kinds of strange food. But guess what—every food he mentions is one that normal people have eaten somewhere in the world!

This is how Edgar, disguised as poor Tom, introduces himself:

Poor Tom; that eats the swimming frog,
the toad, the tadpole, the wall newt, and the
water; that in the fury of his heart, when the
foul fiend rages, eats cow-dung for sallets;
swallows the old rat and the ditch-dog; drinks
the green mantle of the standing pool . . . .

But mice and rats, and such small deer,
Have been Tom's food for seven long year.

— ancient Mexico

— the English once used them for medicine

— animal dung was considered medicine in several lands

— salads

— early America

— algae, similar to seaweed eaten worldwide

— Anasazi

— the Chinese once called rats "household deer"

To eat, oR Not to eat? THat is tHe QuestioN.

RAT STEW
(EARLY EUROPEAN EXPLORERS)

Columbus's son wrote of sailors waiting until dark to eat their biscuits—to keep from seeing the worms crawling in them. A crewman on another explorer's ship told of sailors eating sawdust and sharks when their food ran out.

That was ship life before refrigerators. Every bit of the ship's food spoiled long before the ship could reach shore. If anybody caught a fish it was rotten by the next day. Fortunately, packs of rats lived on ships. Crew members paid the ship's rat catcher high prices for rats because that was the best food they had left!

SEAFOOD MAKES ME SICK

after eight weeks at sea
the rats start looking good

diced small   drowned in gravy
they almost pass for food

we shut our eyes and try to think
one word
                    "venison"

TiMe FoR Ye OLD PoEM

COMe 'eRe, fisHy.

Great Rat Cooking Starts with Quality Rats

The world's most famous dictionary of French food says that meat from a well-fed rat can be quite good—despite an occasional musky flavor. In fact, the people who made barrels for France's wine loved to eat a good quality rat. They grilled rats grown fat on fine Bordeaux wine, using broken barrels for fuel.

Venison is deer meat. A European sailor might well have tried to imagine this NoBLE food in his stew—since eating it was often illegal in his homeland.

The World of Rodents International Dining Club

Some ancient Chinese ate live baby rats, while ancient Romans relished stuffed dormouse (a tree-climbing rat relative). South America's Incas ate guinea pigs, and invading Europeans liked them too.

But it wasn't just the ancients who enjoyed a steaming bowl of rodent stew. Many Americans today eat squirrels—cousins to the furry heroes who saved sailors with their meat and made emperors call for more.

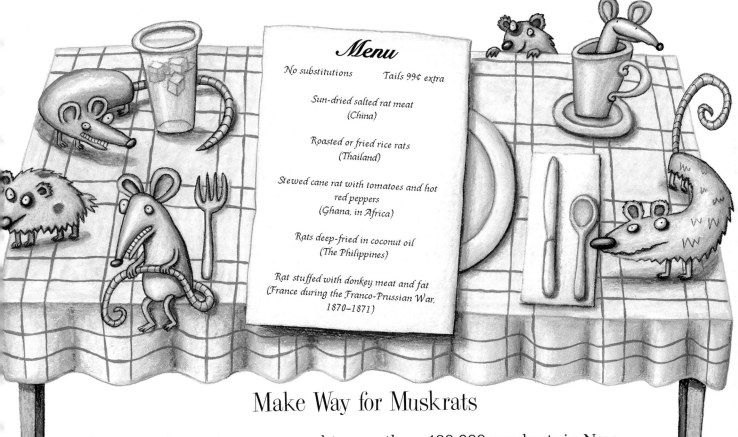

Menu

No substitutions   *Tails 99¢ extra*

Sun-dried salted rat meat
(China)

Roasted or fried rice rats
(Thailand)

Stewed cane rat with tomatoes and hot
red peppers
(Ghana, in Africa)

Rats deep-fried in coconut oil
(The Philippines)

Rat stuffed with donkey meat and fat
(France during the Franco-Prussian War,
1870–1871)

Make Way for Muskrats

In a recent year, trappers caught more than 400,000 muskrats in New Jersey alone. Most trappers threw away the meat and sold the fur for a few dollars.

What a waste! One adventurous trapper compared muskrat's flavor to beef, and said he preferred it to rabbit. Muskrat is a traditional food in parts of Canada and Cajun country.

What's worse than starving on a rat-infested ship?

Being a rat on a ship full of starving people.

FRIED ROBINS ON TOAST

(COLONIAL AND CIVIL WAR AMERICA)

Robins probably were never on America's list of top ten food birds, but they were once among the contenders. Both Native Americans and colonists enjoyed a plump spring robin for breakfast.

A British official reported in about 1840 that people of the United States ate "little birds of all descriptions." So it's no surprise that fried robins on toast appeared in American breakfasts as recently as the Civil War.

Today, the Migratory Bird Treaty Act of 1918 protects all wild birds except game birds like ducks and geese.

Is it just me, or does something smell pretty good?

time for a Hot New Poem.

CAPTAIN'S DELIGHT

early each morning all of his life
captain john barker's capable wife

fried up four robins she'd fixed in a pan
to serve on toast to her stout little man

so that good captain john could travel about
and call for his men with a jolly shout

—thus barker's militia, that merry band,
was built on red robins fried in a pan

Don't Forget to Pluck Them First!

Recipes like this one from 1859 had to be vague because cooks had no way of knowing how hot the fire was. Captain John probably ate half-raw robin more than once in his life.

Birds on Toast

Pick and draw them very carefully, salt and dredge with flour, and roast over a quick fire ten or fifteen minutes. Serve on toast with butter and pepper. You can put in each one an oyster dipped in butter and then in bread crumbs before roasting. They are also very nice broiled.

RECIPE BOX

Pigeon Madness

The passenger pigeon was probably the most abundant bird ever to appear on the earth. Millions of birds often blocked out the sun and turned day to night. Yet an army of hunters wiped the passenger pigeon out in only a few decades. Hunters sometimes netted five hundred passenger pigeons at a time. One tiny town in Michigan shipped out at least seven million dead birds a day during part of 1869.

When the birds became rare, hunters went after them even harder. Pigeon meat had grown into a huge industry, and pigeon traders still needed to make a living. Soon the birds couldn't even settle down to nest because people shot them every place they landed. The last passenger pigeon died in 1914.

Some Popular American Foods of 1776

Soup with Marigold petals

Pigs' feet

Squirrel Pie

Milkweed Shoots

Dandelion Salad

Pickled Passenger Pigeons

Opossum Stew

Raspberry Leaf Tea

MR. Audubon—What bird do you Like Best?

A Woodcock, Lightly Roasted, with a jug of Newark cider.

PART THREE
If You Think That's Sick, Look in Your Fridge
Strange Stories from Your Own Kitchen

MILK
(MOST COUNTRIES)

When cows chew grass and weeds, they swallow the food into the first two of four stomachs. Then the cows burp the grass up, chew some more, and send the mush through the other two stomachs to make milk (see diagram). Last of all, milk comes out through the udder—which is like a giant sweat gland. How could something so awful be so good?

Now HeRe's a Moooving poem.

HOPE THERE'S NO FUR IN IT

cows make it trickle out
people make it chocolate

(black widows don't
make
it) too busy
spinnakering
around

mine comes from the store
in a fat plastic jug

How Much of Your Milk Is Fat?

Hooded Seal 61%
(the highest known of any animal)

Blue Whale 41%
(world's largest animal)

Bottlenose Dolphin 29%

Reindeer 11%

Human 4%

Cow 4%

Black Rhinoceros .2%
(the lowest known of any animal)

HONEY
(WORLDWIDE)

If milk is juice from a huge hairy beast, then honey is juice from a tiny one. Fuzzy bees suck sweet flower juice to bring back to the hive. There, bees pass this nectar around with their tongues till it starts to thicken. Bees' bodies squirt a chemical into the nectar to help change it to honey. After puking it into the honeycomb, the bees fan it with their wings till it's just the right thickness.

To many Ethiopians, the best honey has the honeycomb and grubs (baby bees) in it.

From the Land of Milk and Honey

Here's a recipe made mostly of bee sugar and cow squirt. It is one of the most delicious desserts ever invented—ice cream!

Roses are Red, Violets are blue, I have to find Nectar, but here's a poem for you.

HOPE THEY STRAIN THE STINGERS OUT

bees keep it in their combs
people keep it in their homes

(bears don't
keep
it) too busy
berrying
around

mine goes on bread
and tastes best soaked in

Chocolate Honey Banana Smash Ice Cream
(Makes enough for three kids)

1 LARGE BANANA, PEELED
1/2 CUP WHIPPING CREAM
1/3 CUP MILK
2 TABLESPOONS HONEY
2 1/2 TEASPOONS CHOCOLATE SYRUP

1. In a bowl, smash the banana to a pulp. Squish it into a 1/2 cup container and eat the leftover pulp. 2. Stir in the other stuff. 3. Cover and put the glop in the freezer. Lick the spoon. 4. Set a timer for three hours. 5. After three hours, check to see if the goo needs stirring. If it seems too hard around the edges, smush it up a little. Put it back in the freezer. Check after another hour and smush again, if needed. When it looks and tastes ready, it is. The whole thing takes at least four hours—and if you leave the stuff in the freezer much longer it will get too hard. NOTE: Do not serve to children under one year old. Eating honey sometimes makes babies very sick.

CHEESE

(MOST COUNTRIES)

Cheese happens when certain germs (called *bacteria*) and/or chemicals act on milk. Bacteria make your feet stink and give cheese its odor. Some of the bacteria in cheese are the same as the ones that live in your body to help digest food.

Cheese makers use an enzyme from animals' stomach linings to curdle milk. Then they drain off the liquid, leaving behind *curd*, the first stage in a cheese's life. As the bacteria grow and spread, they give different kinds of cheese their special flavors.

TIME FOR A POEM THAT, WELL... STINKS!

THE THING IN THE BACK OF THE REFRIGERATOR

slimy as worms
made by germs
grows green fur
sharp as a burr
stinks like feet
worse in the heat
don't call it cheese

it's a milk disease

Cottage cheese takes less than a day to make. Cheddar takes at least three months, and Parmesan can take more than two years. When does cheese taste best?

When it's in my mouth.

Cheese: Eat It Alive!

Hi! We're the little guys that make cheese! Have us for dinner!

That's right! When you eat many types of cheese, you eat the bacteria that helped make it. Not only are these bacteria harmless, some are even good for you.

Question: How many bacteria live in one bite of cheese?

Answer: One mouthful can hold over a trillion bacteria—almost two hundred times the total number of people in the world.

That's a Lot of Cheeseburgers

Americans eat more than three and half million tons of cheese a year. Look what you could do if you cornered the U.S. market on cheese:

Make a pizza that would cover all of New York City

Give thirty pounds of cheese to every rat in America

Build an actual-size replica of the Great Pyramid of Giza (with some left over for lunch)

Build a cheese wall six feet high and one foot thick around Texas

Cheese is just milk with a bad attitude.

Hardly. Milk is merely cheese lacking culture.

FUNGUS

(WORLDWIDE)

From the mushrooms on your pizza and the yeast in its crust to the mildew behind the sink, fungi are everywhere.

In fact, there are millions of fungi in your house that you never even say "hi" to! You breathe them in every breath, and they grow in your food.

Fungi are especially easy to find in damp places—in the forest, on dead bugs, or between your toes when you get athlete's foot. Many wild fungi are poisonous, but mushrooms from the store are edible and delicious.

AND NOW FOR a POEM.

GUESS I BETTER CLEAN THE GREEN STUFF OUT FROM BEHIND THE SINK

Help! There's fungus on my chocolate cake
Help! There's fungus on my T-bone steak

Help! There's fungus on my mom's reflection
Help! There's fungus on my crumb collection

Help! There's fungus in my daydreams
Help! There's fungus on my sunbeams

Next thing you know it'll even be on my double-cheese mushroom pizza

I've even got fungus on my fungus!

CRUMBS

Bread of the Pharaohs

Yeast fungi are so small that four thousand could stand in single file on your thumb. They are much too tiny to see, and yet they're the power behind bread. For bread to rise, the dough has to get a fungus infection. As the yeast grows, it gives off gases that puff the loaf up.

A team of scientists once tried to make bread the way the ancient Egyptians did. Instead of using prepared yeast, they just left their dough out for a week. It rose—and the finished bread was delicious. That's because the air is full of fungus spores and bacteria that can make bread grow.

But using just any old germ in your bread could be dangerous, so people today use a special kind of yeast that's safer and more reliable.

Pigs Like Them, Dogs Like Them, But Me?—
I Think They're Sick

The most expensive mushrooms on earth cost up to $640 a pound. These rare wild fungi—called truffles—grow underground, making them very hard to find. Some animals can smell them while they're still buried. Truffle hunters use pigs and dogs to sniff out these warty globes for us to eat.

TRY a LiTTLe to YoUR LefT.

Do Not Eat!

Here are some common names for deadly poisonous toadstools and their disgusting friends:

AUTUMN SKULLCAP	EARTHSTAR	SHAGGY BEAR
CORPSE FINDER	FAIRY BONNET	SICKENER
DEAD MAN'S FINGERS	FOREST FRIEND	SLIPPERY JACK
DEATH CAP	JACK-O'-LANTERN	STINKY SQUID
DESTROYING ANGEL	POISON PIE	WOLF'S-MILK SLIME

A WEENIE-AND-MARSHMALLOW ROAST

(UNITED STATES)

No one knows when this fall tradition began—burning a perfectly good hot dog over an open fire. Although cave people roasted real dogs ten thousand years ago, and the ancient Greeks loved a good sausage, it wasn't till the twentieth century that the term "hot dog" came into use.

Marshmallows have origins thousands of years old. But early marshmallows hardly resembled the incendiary puffballs of today. Like most traditions, our modern custom of the marshmallow-and-weenie roast is a stew of old and new.

...And now a poem.

AUTUMN RITUAL

When the pumpkins leer
by every door
and the candy bags groan
with sweet-tooth gore

then fires must play!
and leaves must turn!
marshmallows must blaze
—and the weenies burn!

There's No Mallow in Marshmallow

Marshmallows get their name from a swamp plant called the *marsh mallow*. Early marshmallow makers molded these treats one at a time, using mallow root as their main ingredient. Today, factories squirt out long marshmallow snakes to be chopped into the sweet pillows that we love to eat.

These snakes no longer contain mallow (they're made with gelatin instead), but marshmallows still make a perfect match for a well-burnt weenie. Maybe that's because gelatin comes from the skin and bone of pigs or cows.

Hot Dog Days and Chili Dog Nights

So the baked bats of Samoa scare you. And France's stuffed calf eyeballs stare up accusingly from your plate. Then why are you biting into that tube of pulverized meat scraps?

Every meat wiener once mooed, snorted, or cackled—before high-speed choppers whipped it as smooth as cake batter. A machine squirted this batter into long bags (later stripped off by another machine) to be pinched into franks, smoked, and cooked.

Fifty million hot dogs disappear daily into American mouths. In one season alone, five billion tubes of pink jiggly meat vanish with a gulp repeated throughout the land. That's enough to loop a chain of hot dogs fifteen times around the earth.

With so many wieners disappearing, there ought to be room at our bonfires for some more exotic meat. After all, those french-fried eyeballs came from the same animal as your frankfurter.

Eat a frog,
save a wiener—
Leaner·Cleaner·Greener!

Halloween Monsters

These all-time monstrosities set the record just by showing up. But the real scare is when your mom says you have to eat the whole thing!

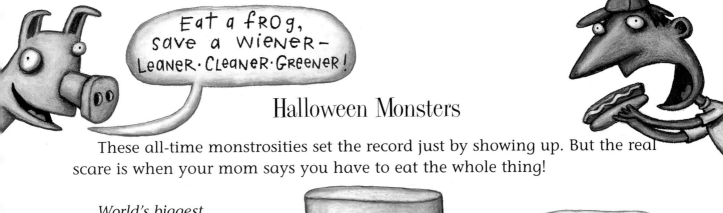

World's biggest . . .

PUMPKIN
990 pounds
Ashton, Ontario
1994

MARSHMALLOW
671 pounds
Ligonier, Indiana
1993

SINGLE PIECE
OF CANDY
4,078 ¹/₂ pounds
Diemen, Netherlands
1990

SAUSAGE
28.77 miles long
Kitchener, Ontario
1995

POPCORN BALL
2,225 pounds
Sac County, Iowa
1995

What do you call
a jack-o-lantern
carved from a
hot dog?

A hollow
weenie!

YOU ARE EATING SCIENCE FICTION

Imagine: travel back fifty years or more and think of what your life would have been like if you had lived long ago.

In most towns before 1950 there were no fast-food restaurant chains. There were no marshmallow cereals, no frozen pizzas, and no microwave dinners. To most people, eating food zapped with rays in a cardboard box would have seemed like science fiction. Maybe even scary—or disgusting!

Now: travel fifty years into the future. What will you eat when you are a grandparent?

Will you eat yeast burgers with bug sauce instead of cow-and-ketchup sandwiches? How about shark fin soup in a city under the sea? Or maybe a delicate fungus that grows only on space station ventilators!

The food of the future might come from a lab, or it might come from the most humble thing on earth—a mealworm.

Mealworms are free, abundant, great tasting, and nutritious. Why shouldn't they be your favorite food?

After all, they're the perfect excuse not to eat your spinach.

See you in the future, kids!

Can't think of a better place to meet than that.

I sure hope there's a banana burger in my future.

IT'S DISGUSTING—AND YOU CAN READ IT!

Read these books to learn even more about the weird foods people eat. Books written especially for kids are marked with a !, but the grown-up books are good too.

PEOPLE EAT THE WILDEST THINGS

Chang, K. C., editor. *Food in Chinese Culture.* New Haven: Yale University Press, 1977.
! Downer, Lesley. *Japanese Food and Drink.* New York: The Bookwright Press, 1988.
! George, Jean Craighead. *The Wild, Wild Cookbook.* New York: HarperCollins, 1982.
! Lovett, Sarah. *Extremely Weird Frogs.* Santa Fe: John Muir Publications, 1991.
Madlener, Judith Cooper. *The Sea Vegetable Book.* New York: Clarkson N. Potter, 1977.
Taylor, Ronald L. and Barbara J. Carter. *Entertaining with Insects.* Santa Barbara, California: Woodbridge Press, 1976.

FROM MAMMOTH MEATBALLS TO SQUIRREL STEW

! Aliki. *A Medieval Feast.* New York: HarperCollins, 1983.
! Arnold, Caroline. *The Ancient Cliff Dwellers of Mesa Verde.* New York: Clarion Books, 1992.
Lister, Adrian, and Paul Bahn. *Mammoths.* New York: Macmillan, 1994.
! Penner, Lucille Recht. *The Colonial Cookbook.* New York: Hastings House, 1976.
! Penner, Lucille Recht. *A Native American Feast.* New York: Simon & Schuster Books for Young Readers, 1994.
! Simon, James. *Ancient Rome* (Eyewitness Books). New York: Alfred A. Knopf, 1990.

IF YOU THINK THAT'S SICK, LOOK IN YOUR FRIDGE

! Cobb, Vicki. *Science Experiments You Can Eat.* New York: HarperCollins, 1954.
! Illsley, Linda. *Cheese.* Minneapolis: Carolrhoda Books, 1991.
! Ontario Science Center. *Foodworks.* Reading, Massachusetts: Addison-Wesley, 1987.
! Penner, Lucille Recht. *The Honey Book.* New York: Hastings House, 1980.

SELECT BIBLIOGRAPHY

Anderson, E. N. *The Food of China.* New Haven: Yale University Press, 1988.

Austin, Thomas, ed. *Two Fifteenth-Century Cookery Books.* London: N. Trubner & Co. for the Early English Text Society, 1888.

Brothwell, Don and Patricia. *Food in Antiquity.* New York and Washington: Frederick A. Praeger, 1969.

Digby, Bassett. *The Mammoth.* London: H. F. & G. Witherby, 1926.

Ferguson, William M. and Arthur H. Rohn. *Anasazi Ruins of the Southwest in Color.* Albuquerque: The University of New Mexico Press, 1987.

Ford, Barbara. *Future Food: Alternate Protein for the Year 2000.* New York: Morrow, 1978.

Hammond, P.W. *Food and Feast in Medieval England.* London: Alan Sutton Publishing, 1993.

Hendrickson, Robert. *More Cunning Than Man.* New York: Stein and Day, 1983.

Hieatt, Constance B. and Sharon Butler, eds. *Curye on Inglysch.* London: Oxford University Press for the Early English Text Society, 1985.

Luchetti, Cathy. *Home On the Range.* New York: Villard Books, 1993.

Montagné, Prosper. *Larousse Gastronomique.* New York: Crown Publishers, 1961.

Pigafetta, Antonio. *Magellan's Voyage Around the World.* Edited and translated by James Alexander Robertson. Cleveland: The Arthur H. Clark Company, 1906.

Roberts, David. "Age of Pyramids: Egypt's Old Kingdom." *National Geographic* 187 (1): 2–43. January, 1995.

Schorger, A. W. *The Passenger Pigeon.* Norman: University of Oklahoma Press, 1973.

Schwabe, Calvin W. *Unmentionable Cuisine.* Charlottesville: University Press of Virginia, 1979.

Tannahill, Reay. *Food in History.* New York: Stein and Day, 1973.

Taylor, Ronald L. *Butterflies in My Stomach.* Santa Barbara, California: Woodbridge Press, 1975.

Valli, Eric and Diane Summers. "Nest Gatherers of Tiger Cave." *National Geographic* 177 (1): 106–33. January, 1990.

van der Post, Laurens. *First Catch Your Eland.* New York: Thomas Morrow, 1978.

Wilster, Gustav Hans. *Practical Cheesemaking.* Corvallis: Oregon State University Bookstores, 1969.

Zennie, Thomas M. and C. Dwayne Ogzewalla. "Ascorbic Acid and Vitamin A Content of Edible Wild Plants of Ohio and Kentucky." *Economic Botany* 31 (1): 76–79. January–March, 1977.

INDEX OF FOODS

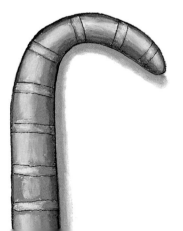